★ ALL-TIME ★ BEST ATHLETES

T0062577

SOCCER SUPERSTARS

ZELDA WAGNER

LERNER PUBLICATIONS ◆ MINNEAPOLIS

Stats are accurate through 2023.

Copyright © 2025 by Lerner Publishing Group, Inc.

All rights reserved. International copyright secured. No part of this book may be reproduced, stored in a retrieval system, or transmitted in any form or by any means—electronic, mechanical, photocopying, recording, or otherwise—without the prior written permission of Lerner Publishing Group, Inc., except for the inclusion of brief quotations in an acknowledged review.

Lerner Publications Company
An imprint of Lerner Publishing Group, Inc.
241 First Avenue North
Minneapolis, MN 55401 USA

For reading levels and more information, look up this title at www.lernerbooks.com.

Main body text set in Mikado.
Typeface provided by HVD Fonts.

Image credits: Keystone-France/Gamma-Keystone/Getty Images, p. 5; George Tiedemann/Sports Illustrated/Getty Images, p. 6; Richard Schultz/WireImage/Getty Images, p. 9; Eric Renard/Icon Sport/Getty Images, p. 10; VI-Images/Getty Images Sport/Getty Images, p. 13; Will Palmer/Allstar/Getty Images Sport/Getty Images, p. 14; David Cannon/Allsport/Hulton Archive/Getty Images, p. 17; Julien Mattia/NurPhoto/Getty Images, p. 18; China News Service/Getty Images, p. 21; Focus On Sport/Getty Images Sport/Getty Images, p. 23. Design elements: FoxGrafy/Shutterstock; Anna Golant/Shutterstock.Cover: AP Photo/Andrew Bershaw/Icon Sportswire.

Designer: Kim Morales

Library of Congress Cataloging-in-Publication Data

Names: Wagner, Zelda, 2000– author.
Title: Soccer superstars / Zelda Wagner.
Description: Minneapolis, MN : Lerner Publications, [2025] | Series: All-time best athletes (Lerner sports rookie) | Includes bibliographical references and index. | Audience: Ages 5–8 | Audience: Grades K–1 | Summary: "Soccer is full of legendary players. But who is the best of the best? Meet the top ten soccer players of all time and the stats that prove their greatness"— Provided by publisher.
Identifiers: LCCN 2023039068 (print) | LCCN 2023039069 (ebook) | ISBN 9798765625750 (library binding) | ISBN 9798765628218 (paperback) | ISBN 9798765632482 (epub)
Subjects: LCSH: Soccer players—Juvenile literature. | Soccer—Records—Juvenile literature.
Classification: LCC GV942.7.A1 W34 2025 (print) | LCC GV942.7.A1 (ebook) | DDC 796.334092/2 [B]—dc23/eng/20230817

LC record available at https://lccn.loc.gov/2023039068
LC ebook record available at https://lccn.loc.gov/2023039069

Manufactured in the United States of America
1-1010187-51909-12/6/2023

TABLE OF CONTENTS

Turn the pages to meet the best soccer players. Count them down from **10** to **1**. Number 1 is the best soccer player ever!

MEET THE 10 BEST SOCCER PLAYERS!

10. ALFREDO DI STÉFANO

Alfredo Di Stéfano played for Real Madrid in Spain. He helped the club be the best in Europe five times.

COUNT IT!
Real Madrid goals:
377

9. FRANZ BECKENBAUER

Franz Beckenbauer was a great defender.

He helped West Germany win the

1974 World Cup.

COUNT IT!

West Germany goals: 14

8. MIA HAMM

At 15, Mia Hamm was the youngest member of the USWNT. She became one of the best scorers in team history.

COUNT IT!
USWNT goals: 158

7. ZINEDINE ZIDANE

Zinedine Zidane won the 1998 World Cup with France. In 2006, he stopped playing. Then he became the coach of Real Madrid.

COUNT IT!

World Player of the Year awards: 3

6. JOHAN CRUYFF

Johan Cruyff played all around the field for the Netherlands. He was great at scoring and defending.

COUNT IT!
Netherlands goals:
33

5. CRISTIANO RONALDO

Cristiano Ronaldo is one of the world's best scorers. Fans love to watch his amazing goals.

COUNT IT!
Real Madrid goals:
450

15

4. DIEGO MARADONA

Diego Maradona helped Argentina win the World Cup twice. He scored 34 total goals for Argentina.

COUNT IT!
Pro club goals: 259

3. MARTA

Marta has been a star for many years. In the 2007 World Cup, she scored seven goals for Brazil. She led Brazil back to the World Cup in 2023.

COUNT IT!

World Player of the Year awards: 6

2. LIONEL MESSI

Lionel Messi has been a winner everywhere he has played. He had his biggest win in 2022. He led Argentina to victory in the World Cup!

COUNT IT!
World Cup goals: 13

1. PELÉ

Pelé could do it all. He was great at shooting and passing. He helped Brazil win three World Cups.

COUNT IT!
Brazil goals: 77

NOW IT'S YOUR TURN.

Who do you think are the best soccer players of all time? Make your own list!

GLOSSARY

club: a soccer team that is not a national team

pro: short for *professional,* to take part in something to make money

USWNT: short for US Women's National Team

World Cup: a soccer contest between teams from different countries

LEARN MORE

Leed, Percy. *Soccer: A First Look.* Minneapolis: Lerner Publications, 2023.

Simons, Lisa M. Bolt. *Curious about Soccer.* Mankato, MN: Amicus, 2024.

Youssef, Jagger. *We Play Soccer!* New York: PowerKids, 2024.

INDEX